Schooling Abraham: Applying Maslow's Hierarchy of Needs to Our Schools

Jon Coley SEd
Or EdS
Whatever floats your boat

Dedicated to all my colleagues through the years. There are so many good things that happen in schools. I see them every day.

Table of Contents

Preface   page 3

Before We Begin   page 7

Chapter 1 Biological Needs   page 11

Chapter 2 Security Needs   page 19

Chapter 3 Relationship Needs   page 29

Chapter 4 Self Respect   page 39

Chapter 5 Self Actualization   page 49

Chapter 6 Why I Wrote This Book   page 53

Chapter 7 So?   page 57

Preface

The only research needed for writing this book was Maslow's Hierarchy of Needs. If you're an educator, you know it well. The problem is that it isn't applied. We in the teaching profession learn about this relatively famous pyramid in developmental psychology courses. We look at it. It makes sense. We take the test. It's pretty much forgotten. From time to time, you may hear about it in some professional development meeting, mentioned in passing. This is merely lip service. After all, you have to make your material look scholarly!

You can do all the research you want. Some of it may help, but many school districts have been driven into the academic ground based on research. There's nothing wrong with data or with being data driven, but if you don't have guidance and application, you're just whistling past the graveyard. It has been said that there are lies, damned lies, and then there are statistics. Well, the same can and should be said about educational research. I've been teaching long enough to know how research works. Most of it is folly. (I'm using nice terms here because I've already used a mild curse word.) Don't get me wrong, there is good research out there, but all research can be, and often is manipulated. I have seen best practices turn around and contradict themselves based on research.

The funny thing is that some good research is often ignored, which brings us back to the hierarchy. It's foundational, easy to understand, and old. It's not the new, cutting edge, fancy, mind boggling stuff that gets people going. To this day I don't know who these people are, but their love of the newest thing has made my job difficult for decades. This book isn't meant as a critique of or as a rant against the academic status quo, though. It's just a look at some of the most useful psychological research ever produced with a few suggestions on how to apply it from a guy who's been teaching for a long time.

As of this writing, I've been teaching nearly twenty-five years. It's been fun. The profession is still a passion for me. That said, I know I won't be doing this forever. Before I retire, I want to give something back to it, something that can make it better. In the Bible, Jesus accused a church of losing its first love (I'm not giving you the verse. Crack that old book open and look for it. It'll do you some good.). He reminded them of what they really needed. I'm not comparing myself to Jesus, here. I'm comparing the American schools to that church. Our first love should be the raising up and edifying of our next generations, the education of our sons and daughters. Most of the time this is lost in a conspiracy of good intentions. Hopefully this writing will cut through all of that and just give some common sense advice on how to make schools better.

Some schools are better than others. I'm not talking about test scores, though they are affected by this too. But when you walk into some schools, the teachers wave at each other as they walk by. The kids are smiling and are happy to be there, for the most part. In short, these schools are nice places to be. If your school is like that, you're blessed and lucky too. There is a good sense of community in the school building. You probably get along with your administrators. Well, this could be any school. All it takes is a little bit of vision, some guidance, and a good attitude.

If you're an administrator and your school isn't like what I described above, it's your fault. Maybe the school was in bad shape when you got there. But have you fixed it yet? Here's the thing. We're all responsible for our school environment, but real change starts and ends with you. I have come to believe that a teacher can read and apply the principles in this book to improve his or her classroom. An administrator, however, can use them to improve the whole school.

Before We Begin

Here's the breakdown. It gives you a completely different feel when you're not looking at the pyramidal diagram. This is my paraphrased, abridged version of the original. I've taken some things out too. Even so, there's a lot to unpack.

Basic Biological Needs - Air, food, drink, shelter, and sleep.
Security Needs - Protection, order, stability, limits.
Relationship Needs - Sense of belonging, affection, group work.
Self Respect - Responsibility, character, achievement.
Self Actualization - Personal growth.

Did you notice anything missing? Let me tell you a funny and completely true story about how even good research can be completely misconstrued. Years ago, in the late 1900's when I first began teaching, there was an uproarious Board of Education meeting in my local school district. Someone had put out a pamphlet and sent it home to ALL THE PARENTS IN THE SCHOOL SYSTEM. It had a cut-and-paste fatal flaw. In small print the pamphlet stated the school professionals are responsible for the safety, academic, emotional, sexual, psychological, and physical needs or the student. It was something like that, but did you catch it? I don't know about you, but I don't want any teacher taking care of my kid's sexual needs. Somehow the person who wrote the pamphlet, the administrators who distributed them, and the teachers who gave them to the kids all missed it.

Now, this was just a foolish mistake, but it illustrates an important point. People don't read research, even good research. It's important to understand what the research really says. I assure you that Maslow was not talking about kids when he listed sexual needs in his hierarchy, so I took it out for this book. If you have a problem with that, there's something really wrong with you. Likewise, if you're an administrator concerned with your teachers' sexual needs, you are in the wrong profession, and probably the wrong location all together. My bet is that a sparse, eight by ten room is in your future. Of course, I'm being facetious here, but it is important to understand what the research is really saying before it's applied. Truth be told, most people just do what they want and use research gobbledegook to back it up.

To finish up this very uncomfortable chapter for me to write, there are some sexual needs in schools that should be addressed. You as a teacher and an administrator are quite responsible for protecting kids from predators. Unfortunately, this happens. The other thing you should consider yourself responsible for is protecting kids from political movements that tend to sexualize children. Your school and classroom should be apolitical, for the most part. That doesn't mean that you can't talk about politics. It does mean, however, that you should watch out for hot button issues that effect kids' lives. There are some political activists who don't mind using children to make their points. Let me just tell you, transgender story time is not okay. Forcing girls to allow boys to shower with them because they identify as girls is unacceptable. If you think it is, you're warped and you need help. To be clear, adults can believe and do whatever they want within the confines of the law. If you are politically active based on your sexuality, fine. Leave kids out of it.

Well, that was no fun. Back to the matter at hand. This book will be divided into five chapters; Basic Biological Needs, Security Needs, Relationship Needs, Self Respect, and Self Actualization. Then there will be two extra chapter wrapping things up. The overall concept is to look at these needs and how they can be met for students, teachers, and for the school as whole. I think these concepts can make your school a better place, so let's get started.

Chapter One - Biological Needs

Air

That shouldn't be a problem. Just don't build schools in the water, right. Not so fast. Kids need to breathe, like everyone else. Since they are under school care for about eight hours a day, they need access to basic medical and first aid care. In other words, a good school should have a competent school nurse. To be fair, this may not be in an administrator's control. If it is in your control, and you decide not to have one, shame on you. I know that hard decisions have to be made. Tax payer money must be spent responsibly. Therefore it must be stated that there is nothing more responsible than promoting and protecting the health of your kids.

Okay, you've got a school nurse. She (he) must be competent. This usually isn't a problem. Ninety-nine out of one hundred nurses are exactly that. What sometimes is a problem is the office set up. The office must have all the basic equipment for a school nurse to operate efficiently and effectively. Also, the school nurse isn't another receptionist or secretary. Don't think you have the right to misuse that position. Administrators have to support the school nurse too. She is charged with the care of your students' health. It is vitally important. Don't get in the way of that.

Give the school nurse a voice. Let her (or him) be empowered to deliver health and hygiene messages to the students and parents. Include her in leadership meetings if at all possible. The school nurse is an important component of the school environment. Treat her (him) that way.

Food and Drink

Let me tell you another story. Long ago, when I was a new and young teacher, our school was overpopulated. Sure it was job security, but we had a lot of classes in every grade level. This wreaked havoc on our lunch schedule. Somehow, because there was little time between the end of the breakfast shift and the first preK lunch shift, the lunchroom staff ate their lunch in the middle of the day. In other words, they stopped serving lunch so they could have lunch! This totally blew my mind. The older kids were eating lunch half an hour later than they would have otherwise. This never should have happened!

Now, I don't wish to disparage the lunchroom staff or the principal involved in this situation. They were just trying to do their best in a tough situation. What I am saying is that the students' Needs were overlooked in this situation. Creative solutions could have been brought t the table. The staff could have rotated their lunch shift a couple of members at a time, instead of all them eating together. Perhaps it was time to go back to the proverbial drawing board and rework the schedule in some way. Luckily this only happened for one school year. Nobody thought it was sustainable, thank goodness.

One thing I believe teachers should consider doing is creating a hungry kid fund, just in case some kids can't afford to buy their lunch. I'm not talking about an ongoing thing here, though. Let's say you're in a school with about fifty teachers. If each teacher donated five dollars to the fund, then that money could be set aside for when kids don't have their lunch money, or have charged to many meals. Food must be made available to all kids during the school day, no matter what.

Finally, I would urge you to be kind to your school's lunchroom staff. They are the busiest restaurant in town, with the rowdiest patrons. Plus, they're not allowed to prepared these meals in a tasty way thanks to foolish federal nutritional standards. They have a big job to do, and it's often quite thankless. Be good to them, they deserve it.

Shelter

I've been lucky enough to work in schools where this hasn't been a problem, for the most part. But it must be said, if your school is a trailer park, the system is letting the kids down. Trailers are sometimes a necessary and temporary solution, but they should not be utilized year after year. This can be a difficult problem to solve logistically speaking, but it can and should be a priority.

Here's an example to show why it's important to get rid of trailers. A special needs class is going about its day. It's a spring afternoon in Georgia. Out of nowhere, the weather turns severe. The teacher and paraprofessionals suddenly have to round up kids, some who cannot walk, some who have to travel slowly, and some who are called "runners" because that's what they do when they panic, and move them from the trailer into the main building. Hard rain, lightning, wind and hail pelting them all the while. This really happened at my school. One of those kids was my daughter. Everything turned out okay, thanks to the dedicated staff working with the kids. But it never should have happened. The system let the school down by allowing its most vulnerable members of the student population to be placed in such a precarious learning environment. I let my daughter down by not saying anything about it in the first place. The system learned its lesson soon after. The special needs class was moved into the building. But if you're a person in charge of anything on the system level, get rid of the trailers as soon as possible!

There's psychological shelter too. Principals should avoid moving teachers around as much as possible. One of the most stressful situations people go through in their lives is the dreaded process of moving. This still applies in the school building. If you're a principal and you like having teachers move around every year for no good reason, stop being a jerk. There is no benefit to this, educational or otherwise. Some people have to move every school year, that's just the way it is, the nature of the beast. That being said, don't cause undue stress for your teachers.

Of course, it's imperative to maintain the school grounds too. This is where a principal can shine. I've worked with two principals that take personal pride in the school building and grounds. Believe me, it makes a difference. Also, if you want to see a successfully maintained school, look at the relationship between the administrator and the school custodian. If they work closely together in tandem, success in this crucial area of schooling is all but guaranteed. An empowered school custodian is the key to having a safe, clean school environment.

Finally, it's the little things. If there's something wrong that you can fix, fix it. For example, a broken playground bench can be fixed with a little know how and elbow grease. If you can't fix it, find someone in the school who can. Kids can and should be involved in keeping the campus clean and safe too. There's nothing wrong with letting them pick up trash on the playground, for instance. Kids need to take ownership in their school's upkeep.

Sleep

Don't worry, I'm not gong to suggest tucking all of your students into bed at night, not even via Zoom, Skype, or GotoMeeting. Nor does this mean you should try work in a daily power nap, unfortunately. Sleep, or lack thereof, should not be ignored. If a student is falling asleep in class repeatedly, you need to find out why. Reprimanding the kid may or may not be the tactic to take. Sure, if the child is staying up too late playing video games, he needs to be held responsible. But there are a plethora of reasons kids lose sleep that are beyond their control. Be nosy, within reason. It is of utmost importance that students are alert and awake while at school. Of course, you should be careful. If you find evidence of abuse or neglect, immediately report that to the school guidance counselor or whomever is designated for such things. Teachers are mandated reporters. Don't forget to be sensitive to the student's need for privacy, though. Confidentiality is a vital teacher ethic that is often violated, usually by accident.

If you're experiencing lack of sleep as a teacher, that's important too. Self care should not be undervalued. Your kids need you to be on top of your game, so to speak.

Take care of yourself! If you're an administrator, you can help your teachers by making the school a sanctuary for all of your faculty and staff. Be someone they can turn to as well as someone they can trust. And, like I said before, don't be a jerk.

Chapter 2 - Security Needs

Protection

We, as educators are expected to protect kids. This has a wide range of applications. Of course, we have to protect them from each other. Bullies are a fact of life. Sometimes we have to protect kids from their home lives, which is incredibly unfortunate. The important thing for teachers and administrators is to be tough and compassionate. It's a hard world out there.

The main day to day form of protection is informational in nature. Kids have to be protected from the media and from online predation. They are able to see God knows what at home, so the school should be a haven away from all of that. This does not mean, however, that kids are shut off from the world at large while in school. They should have a school life rich in media resources. Teachers and media specialists have to work together to maintain a safe cyber space for students. They have to be vigilant.

Rarely, and this is why it gets so much attention, kids have to be protected from teachers. I remember the fair skinned kid who was severely sunburned because his teacher wouldn't let him use sunscreen during a field day for fear of it making the other students sick. This really happened. It was in the news, and it was so stupid and avoidable. I don't know how what this particular teacher could have been thinking, but I do know that other teachers around him should have done something about it. You see, teaching is a profession. One of the hallmarks of professionals it that they police themselves. Teachers, if one of your colleagues is this out of line, tell him or her. Don't let things get out of hand. Like I said before, this is extremely rare. Kids are far safer statistically in schools than anywhere else. Let's keep it that way.

Kids need to be protected from politics. Teachers should be mindful of kids' backgrounds. They should also be aware if there own political persuasions are affecting their lessons. If they are, make sure you are being open and fair about it. You're there to teach, not to be an activist. Also, be aware of what your system is doing. System wide policies have the most potential to be politically tainted. Do what's right. It's not easy, but it's necessary.

The school building itself is the ultimate form of physical protection. The simple act of locking doors will do the most to protect students and staff alike. Teachers should not (I've done this myself in the past) leave doors leading to the outside unlocked. Visitors should have to be checked in through the office. An ounce of prevention is worth a pound of cure.

Here's another story. I was a young child in the second or third grade. We were riding home on the school bus. One of the older kids, at least in middle school, but perhaps in high school, pulled out a pocket knife and held it to my throat. He said, "What you got, son?" Then he pulled it away. He was only playing. He actually showed me the knife and we had a conversation about it. A few days later, one of the lunchroom ladies found out about the incident. I believe my friend and I were discussing it in the cafeteria line. They went to the principal about it. The next thing I knew, I was being questioned about the incident. I told them everything and I'm pretty sure I made it that clear that he was playing, but I never saw that kid again. His sisters still rode the bus with me for years and they never showed any animosity toward me about it.

I told you that story to say this, school is not over until every kid makes it home. The administrators understood that even back in the nineteen eighties. You see, most people have a job in which ninety-nine percent job efficiency is quite good. Schools have to have one hundred percent efficiency on a daily basis. ALL the kids have to get home safely. Anything less is unacceptable. With this in mind, please be kind to bus drivers. They have to get into a cramped metal tube with dozens of unruly passengers of many ages from kindergarten through twelfth grade, and then turn their back on them and drive. If you are an administrator that has the opportunity to make school bus rides safer, do it.

Order and Stability

Kids need structure in their lives, just like the rest of us. Imagine being a six-year-old and walking into a school with kids running around everywhere, yelling at each other, and doing Lord knows what else. You'd be frightened out of your mind. Some kids are scared to death of anything anyway. But if you are escorted into a cozy, comfortable classroom with a friendly teacher overseeing the other kids, you're going to feel a lot better about the whole situation.

While older kids don't need as much guidance as the average kindergartener, the basic need for structure doesn't go away. Kids don't feel safe in a place with no rules. At first, some would love it, but things would soon get too scary for most of them. Students should be expected to walk down the hallways, and not run, skip, jump, push or shove. Students should be expected to clean up after themselves after eating lunch and should not play with their food. It's all hilarious until somebody's favorite shirt gets ruined and they have to show it to their mom later. This is common sense to most people, but imagine a place where the rules are too lax. It does happen from time to time, and it's never a good thing.

Teachers need structure they can depend on in schools too. Here's a story of of catastrophic structural failure. There was a policy, like in many schools, that parents without a tag in the car rider line had to go into the office to sign their child out. A perfectly reasonable policy, but often incomplete. Our school has well over two hundred cars in the line every afternoon. Teachers aren't going to put kids in a car with people they don't know who don't have the right credentials. That's how kids disappear. One of my colleagues had a kindergartner waiting to go home, but the child's parents didn't have the car rider tag. It was a woman driving and a man was her passenger. When my colleague saw that they didn't have a tag, she told them that they would have to go around front into the office to check the child out. She didn't want to, but she had to. There's a long wait time in our car rider line. The man became irate due to the long wait. The child began crying and was escorted down to the office. Then the principal did something I never would have believed. He sent the kid back up to get into the car. Granted, he knew the people, which is mark of a good administrator. They were in fact the child's parents or guardians. But my colleague was left out in the cold, so to speak. She did as she was told and was made to look foolish for it. Well, she didn't look foolish to me or to any other teacher who could possibly be in her shoes in the near future. This did not build trust between the teachers and the administrators.

He should have made them drive down, or asked for their drivers license himself. Then he could have radioed the office to do a check right then. Better yet, the teachers could have been empowered policy wise to ask for an ID at the car and call it in themselves. Instead, a strict policy was put in place and then ignored by the very person whose job it was to make sure everyone carries it out. This never should have happened. Unfortunately, things like this have happened with many different principals at many different schools, though not in such an inglorious fashion, and it's a breach of trust.

It's worse than a lack of trust between two people, which is bad enough. What you do as a school leader to one teacher, you do to all the teachers on that campus. The administrator in the scenario above probably didn't think he was doing anything wrong, I'm sure. He was just probably trying to maintain that one hundred percent job efficiency in the most expedient way possible. But every teacher in our school knew about it by the next day, and they did not forget it either. Principals, back up your teachers in all areas. They have to know that they can trust you. If they can't, you are worthless as a leader and your school will suffer for it.

It's important to note that this principle in the hierarchy can be easily misapplied. If you put too many rules on people, that's called micromanaging. Some of you may be thinking that it's a fine line. This is absolutely not true. If you are an administrator who's into adding rules, regulations, or procedures because you like things done a certain way, then you are a micromanager and nobody likes you for one simple reason. You enjoy having your own needs met instead of meeting the needs of your staff. In short, you are exasperating. The Bible specifically tells fathers not to exasperate their children. Use this wisdom in a professional setting as well. The same goes for teachers with their students too. Those of you who have to fortify complex psychological structures in the form of class rules and push them on your students are wasting your time as well as your kids' time. Teachers, don't exasperate your students. Just kidding about nobody liking you, by the way.

Limits

Kids need limits. They don't have to be strict, but they do have to be. Teachers know the following phrase all too well. "Well, can we ..." Kids naturally push boundaries. It's part of growing up. When teachers discuss rules with kids, and they feel comfortable enough to ask, they are going to try to find out what they can get away with. The important thing isn't to spell out to the Nth degree the exact rule to the exact letter. It is of far more importance to be consistent with kids. If you're not, students won't know what to expect from you on a daily basis. They won't know which teacher (that happens to have your face) they are going to get. These kids basically live with you for a whole year, and that's no way to live.

Flexibility is important too. This is not contradictory to what's written above. The metaphor of a backbone is the best illustration of this. It can bend, but it's strong and hard. So if a kid who is usually well behaved accidentally breaks the rules, it's okay to relent a little. But that kid who continually breaks the rules on purpose may need to have his/her world come crashing down (a little hyperbole here). Be a teacher with backbone.

The same concept of limits applies to administrators, with the caveat that you are now dealing with adults who can (and should) put you in your place too. There are limits you should uphold in the school consistently. This usually applies in supporting teachers and assistant teachers (paraprofessionals), especially with maintaining order outside the classroom. Be sure not to put them in powerless situations. Help maintain school wide expectations and your faculty and staff (there's a difference) will reciprocate. You will be appreciated for it. Yes, there are your own professional limits and preferences in the office you get to maintain too, but don't get the big head. A leader and a boss are two different things.

Now, some tough love for administrators. I was hesitant to write this, but it's important. Most teachers, both historically and currently, are women. For some reason, many principals have been men. There are many female administrators today, but this precept still holds. Administrators, if you're talking to a room full of women, be sure that what you say and how you say it is the same thing you would say in front of their husbands, whether they have them or not. If this is not the case, shut up and go back to the drawing board. I'm not saying that you can't discuss difficult things. I'm not even saying you're not the one in charge. I am saying to watch yourself. Be professional.

Chapter 3 - Relationship Needs

Sense of Belonging

This is your chance to make a difference in kids' lives. Give them a sense of belonging. It doesn't have to be complicated. But it is important to note that I'm not talking about your attitude as a teacher or administrator, yet. The school itself should be an environment that fosters a sense of community from all common areas on campus to each and every classroom. Kids and adults alike should be able to feel a sense of welcome whenever on the school grounds. The administrator has the most influence on the school at large. The teacher has incredible influence on the kids in each classroom.

The building should be well maintained. Nothing is less welcoming than a shoddy looking building, or as unsafe. It should be clean too. Moreover, the building's decor should be age appropriate. Bright colors and fun decorations should be all over elementary school walls. The school should be a fun place for kids to look at. Middle schools should have "Cooler" decor. The colors may be a little more muted, but there should still be plenty of age appropriate decorations that kids and adults can enjoy. High schools would be more modern and iconic. This is a very different practice for learning institutions. Psychologists studied color a few decades ago and found that muted colors affected behavior. It had a calming effect on kids. This is probably true, but the drab colors of school walls have been unwelcoming and depressing for years and years. I believe that the need to control inadvertently took precedence over the need to foster a sense of belonging. Make the school building a place you would like to see every day. It's worth it.

School Spirit should not be underestimated. This can go a long way in fostering a sense of belonging. It, above all, must be authentic. This should be across the board too. Sports are important, but all aspects of school life should be involved. Any given school should represent the community with the best it has to offer, their young people. With this in mind, school spirit becomes entrenched in community spirit, a formidable combination. Administrators and teachers, be cheerleaders for your students. Celebrate their accomplishments with them too.

The only way to get buy in from the kids in this area is to really mean it. The administrators and teachers should value and talk about school spirit on a daily basis with their students. If it's truly important to you, it will become important to the kids too. This will foster a sense of belonging that will last a lifetime.

Here's another story that should illustrate this point. I was in a grade level meeting and another teacher who was t present was brought up. It wasn't gossip. The conversation was concerning his teaching practices. This teacher worked his kids hard and got a lot out of them academically even though he taught a very young grade level. Well, I knew something about him that the other teachers and administrators didn't. You see, we went to the same school in the town just north from where we were teaching. I've always known that my school had higher academic requirements than the surrounding schools in the area. I don't know how it happened, but I know it to be true. So I spoke up and told my colleagues that he teaches this way because of where we went to school. Yes, a middle aged man, who never even thinks that much about his middle school or high school experience, was still affected by school spirit.

One tried and true method of community building that fosters a sense of belonging has come under fire in the past few decades, competition. For some reason, people think that just because there are winners and losers, students shouldn't compete. The truth is that kids need to learn how to be generous winners and resilient losers. Life is hard. Competition is a way for kids to build themselves up for it. Granted, there are some things that shouldn't be turned into a competition, but it's okay to have contests. They build character.

Affection

We all need it, some of us more than others. The main thing in schools is to be authentic. Kids know when you are being duplicitous. They may not know your reasons or have the vocabulary to explain it, but they can sense it. Be authentic with kids and be yourself. Remember, kind words spoken honestly with a pat on the back are much better than a hug given begrudgingly. Kids know a fake smile when they see one too. Don't be a Delores Umbridge. If you don't get that reference, you really need to get out more.

Adults should remember to be authentic with each other too, teachers and administrators alike. If you don't like a coworker's dress, don't give her a fake compliment on it. Look at each other's work. Find out what works for them, then give them the ultimate compliment, ask them how they do it. Try to do something like it in your own classroom. That's authenticity, and it's as good as gold.

Humor is a great way to foster a sense of belonging. You don't have to be a comedian. Just lighten up a little. It's okay to laugh, even in front of kids. If a kid feels comfortable enough to tell you a joke, that kid has a sense of belonging. By the way, what's invisible and smells like bananas? Monkey farts! A kid told me that joke, and its hilarious. If you don't think so, I don't think there's any hope for you.

The only other thing, to my mind, is to recommend that teachers look out for those kids who are falling through the cracks. The ones who suffer quietly. Usually kids who have difficult home lives are the ones that show out in class. They certainly need compassion, but there are many troubles to be had in this world. Look out for those kids flying under the radar too. You don't have to be nosy. In fact, you shouldn't, but you should ask kids how they are doing. Make time to talk with your students. Shoot the breeze with them. Share some of your life with them. These days, school life is all nose to the grindstone. And woe unto you if you "waste" one single second of instructional time. The truth is, however, that a kid cannot be well instructed with the weight of the world on his/her shoulders. It's a sad fact that sometimes it is.

Administrators, this need applies to you too, though not in the way you may think. Teachers, in all likelihood, don't need constant praise and pats on the back, but lack of warmth from administrators can do big damage to school morale. By this I don't mean that having a dry personality makes you a bad leader. As my wife likes to say, "You be you, Boo." Decisions you make can affect this human need. Uh oh, I feel another story coming on.

Just a few years ago, some of our school's leadership came up with an idea, a tea party. Our district teacher surveys indicated that the majority of us wanted to understand more about our colleagues' practices. We were given a sheet of paper with a picture of a tea glass. Our task was the take some of our planning time and observe another teacher. Then we were to write down our observations. At the very bottom of the tea glass, where the dregs would be, we were to write down any problems observed during the lesson. In other words, we were being ordered to rat out our colleagues! Then we were going to have small group meetings and "spill the tea" about what we saw.

In short, there was no way in Hades I was going to do this. It just wasn't right. I observed one of my colleagues and described her lesson, but the bottom of the tea glass I wrote that I would never fill this bottom part out and that this assignment was the product of bad leadership. Yeah, I probably shouldn't have done that. But I wasn't alone! Most of the teachers, I learned via word of mouth, did not fill out that bottom part. They were smarter about it than I was. They just left it blank. The tea was never spilled.

To clarify things here, the administrators doing this were given a bad, or unclear, assignment from their higher ups and just wanted to do something to address the situation that wouldn't take up too much of their faculty's time. They thought that it was a cute way to do it too. I mean, who doesn't like tea? Here's the real question, though. How much warmth do you think the teachers felt when they were given this assignment at the beginning of the year during a long, grueling faculty meeting? If the administrators, who were just as swamped as all the teachers at the time, had a guide like the hierarchy of needs, they would have seen that this activity in no way fostered warmth and affection in the school. Quite the opposite, actually. To their credit, they realized this quickly and dropped it like the poop covered rock it was. The assignment was revamped in a much more palatable way that all the faculty could get behind.

Group Work

This is a part of education that has gotten better in spades over the last few decades. With the furniture literally bolted to the floor, the concept of working in groups was very much lacking in the first hundred years of education. Fortunately, that has changed completely. Group work, like centers, is common practice today, and in quite innovative ways too. It's one of the few changes that I, an old hat teacher, embrace whole heartedly. I would say that good old fashioned seat work is still okay, though. It still has its place. Not every lesson should be a center. I dare say that most teachers know this and instruct accordingly. If you have trouble designing lessons around centers, look around your school and ask. There are plenty of teachers with great ideas that they put into practice every day.

There is one place where group work is being harmed on the national level, kindergarten. Gone are the days of social games and activities where young people learn important skills like taking turns and getting along with others. Kids need learning stations such as play kitchens, toy construction sites, building blocks, and mini gyms inside the classroom. Moreover, they need about one hour of free play outside daily, which could be broken up into two or three recesses. This is real learning. Don't let anybody tell you otherwise. The other pencil and paper learning cannot truly take place without this as a foundation.

Instead, teachers are forced to make their little ones practice the first one hundred sight words, the alphabet, and math skills almost all day long. One argument for this is that kids can learn them. They have the ability. Well, many can, but that doesn't mean that they should. They can learn how to get along together and work in groups too, but they are not because somebody thought a kindergarten class looks better with six year olds slaving away at a desk all day. Basic letter and number skills should definitely be taught. Sight words are important to learn for those kids who are ready. I'm in no way arguing against that. But too much of the school day is focused on this, and the one size fits all policy doesn't really fit anyone. Whomever came up with the current kindergarten curricula must have never heard of Maslow's Hierarchy of Needs. It blows my mind that it's a nation wide trend. It's a shame too.

Chapter 4 - Self Respect

Some of you with a sharper eye may have already noticed that I did something a little suspicious here. Perhaps I should explain myself. It is true that Maslow's Hierarchy listed self esteem as its fourth tier in the pyramid. I changed this to self respect because that's really what he was talking about. There may be some academic weirdo having a coronary right now, but this book is about practicality, not theory. If you're talking about character, responsibility and achievement, you're not talking about the self esteem promoted in schools today thanks to those aforementioned academic weirdos and pop psyche idiots (sorry not sorry) in the media. You're talking about self respect. That's completely different.

Educational psychologists have been promoting self esteem for decades. This is where the phenomenon of the participation trophy comes in. It's where we get little kids being encouraged to feel special because they have two eyes, two feet, and two hands. Well, they are not special. In fact, the I'd call the kid with only one foot, one hand, or one eye special. That's a kid who's building character. The concept of self esteem has become completely adulterated. It's nothing like its original meaning. I don't know how it happened. You'd think experts would be able to read the research they are promoting and foisting on society at large. If you object to this, just remember that prisons are loaded with convicted felons filled with heaps of self esteem. If that's your future vision for your kids, keep on with the self esteem quackery. It isn't mine. That's why I'm using the term, "Self Respect."

Responsibility

Responsible people recognize and react to needs outside of themselves and can be trusted to address them. The younger you are, the smaller your responsibilities, which is reasonable and necessary. All kids, however, can and should be taught responsibility.

Responsibility can be and usually is fostered in the classroom. Kids need to take ownership in the upkeep of the classroom, even at the kindergarten level. Ninety-nine of one hundred teachers know this instinctively. They have kids who wipe down the desks daily or weekly. Some designated helpers sweep the classroom floors whether or not custodians come in to clean the floor at night. Kids are selected to put away supplies, or maybe the whole class does it as they work. The good news is that kids want to be helpful. It's hardwired in their brains. The funny thing is that if you take the laziest kid at home and put him in the classroom, he/she can magically become a super helpful hard worker. Sorry parents, it's just life.

The one tip I would give to new teachers, because old hats like myself have been doing this for years, is to give that troublesome kid special responsibilities. It really helps. Again, be authentic. Make sure an actual classroom need is being fulfilled. In this, you will be meeting some the child's psychological needs too.

Teachers go into the job knowing that it's a big responsibility. This focus is almost always on the kids, which is just fine in and of itself. There are other responsibilities teachers have too, though. It's important that teachers are responsible for each other. They must work as a team, usually by grade levels. Don't let your team members down. Do your part. Team leaders, don't exasperate your colleagues. Make sure your meetings are necessary and kept as short as possible. Teacher teams, find ways to get past personality conflicts. That can be easier said than done, but it is important. One piece of advice, don't take grudges home with you. It's not worth it. If there's a problem, hash it out as soon as possible. Don't let it fester, because that's exactly what it will do, and you will regret it. Too many teachers lose sleep over personality conflicts and hurt feelings. If someone is crossing a line with you, let her/him know. Its unpleasant, but not as unpleasant as stewing in it. Look at it this way. If you're letting a personality conflict bother you, it will affect your work. Don't let it, because it is your responsibility to be at your best for your students as much as possible every single day.

Administrators have the most responsibility in the school. Shocking, I know. An entire book can be written about this alone. Most teachers would be surprised at how many toilets their principals have to clean and unclog on a daily basis. This is just to illustrate the scope of administrator responsibilities. They do far more that what you would expect. Teachers, if you have good administrators, and you know if you do, appreciate them.

Administrators, unfortunately a big part of your job is delivering bad news to your teachers. You have to "waste their time" with the new policies that are going to be crammed down their throats. You have to ensure that the newest scheme coming from the higher ups is being implemented, whether it's good or not. It comes with the job. Be sensible and compassionate. If you have a "my way or the highway" attitude, that strategy will always backfire on you. You are a part of the team too. Be a leader, not a boss, and your team will always make you look good for it.

Now, an opinion nobody asked for. According to best practices, one big responsibility of all the school administrators is to be the instructional leaders of the school. I don't know how this became a best practice, because it's an incredibly stupid idea. First of all, it contradicts the bottom up approach found in the other best practice precepts. That's not the main problem, though. Administrators are often placed in charge of schools, like an elementary school, even though they were something else, like a high school PE teacher beforehand. In other words, they are in charge of a bunch of classroom teachers even though they have never done the job themselves. This practice is actually just fine. A healthy variety of backgrounds is generally a good thing. While it is perfectly okay to do this, these people have no business being the instructional leaders of a school if they have never been the ones to deliver said instruction. This is just a little hang up I have as a teacher, but I'm not the only one. Administrators, don't be foolish enough to think you can tell teachers how to do their jobs if you have never done it yourself. They will never respect you in that capacity if they take their profession seriously. Most teachers take their jobs very seriously, by the way. This doesn't mean that you can't be a good administrator, you just need a little humility in that area. Humility, confidence properly placed, is a hallmark of a responsible person and of a good leader.

Achievement

This section has nothing to do with standardized testing. High stakes testing is a reality, and teachers should hope for and encourage the best possible scores from their kids. But people must realize that this kind of testing is a racket, literally. It's just a way for state governments and federal agencies to use the taxpayers' money to award companies huge contracts for tests, then to use the scores, good or bad, as impetus to have more testing from the companies. Meanwhile these companies donate to politicians, and the cycle continues. Feel free to disagree with me about this. You'll be wrong, but absolutely, feel free.

Achievement is a daily occurrence than comes only from diligent work. Teachers know this. It can be marked by quizzes, tests, projects, and slate of all kinds of academic tools. The most important sense of achievement, however, comes from within. Researchers like Alfie Kohn are big proponents of this concept. They are not wrong, but they are also not practical. Teachers don't have the power to dive into someone's mind or heart. There's this thing called free will, and it's inalienable to the human condition. Instead outer motivations and learning opportunities must be provided. Kids need encouragement, and achievement should be valued and appreciated throughout the school. The more encouragement, the better. This is the only way to spark that inner fire. All kids want to achieve at something. Give them the chance.

School wide achievement should be encouraged and recognized too. What in the world is wrong with being the cleanest school in the state? The best cafeteria? Administrators can provide achievement opportunities for students, faculty, and staff alike. School wide reading or writing contests are great to have. Math and science competitions are fantastic. Special programs showing off student talents in art, music, or performance are great. There are state and national awards for schools that achieve ranging from debate to PE and everything in between.

Again, authenticity is vitally important. Recognition of achievement is an integral part of school life, but it can go too far. Here's another story from my teaching experience years ago. Our school had a program that recognized student achievement quarterly, which was way too much in my opinion. Once or twice a year is plenty. Nevertheless, we had awards ceremonies every nine weeks. The awards included Most Improved and Citizenship, which are just fine. In fact, I believe those two awards are more important than the academic ones. This is where it all went wrong in my too old to care opinion. The academic awards included, All A's, All A's and B's, and All Passing. BIG mistake. Kids should never be rewarded for C's and rarely be rewarded for B's.

To be fair, this practice came from a good place, the desire not to leave any kids out. If achievement is a real human need, however, it should be recognized authentically. Giving kids rewards and recognition for C's is far from authentic. It's a little pat on the back that says, "That's okay, we know you couldn't do any better." To add insult to injury, there were prizes attached to the awards. These were, in a word, junk. They were fun, and that's good, but I suspect that achievement was equated with junk in the minds of some of the kids. Even worse, some of the All A's kids thought the prizes in the All Passing category were better. The prizes should have at least been accumulative in nature.

Now here's the big, stinky elephant in the room. The educators did exactly the opposite of what they intended. They lavished prizes on most of the kids hoping with bleeding hearts (a little mean of me) not to leave anyone out. Well, what about the kids who made F's? They were definitely left out. Usually this was no more than one or two kids in a class. How do you think they felt when everyone else got prizes? Do you think they felt motivated or alienated? The truth is that they didn't deserve a prize, the All Passing kids didn't deserve a prize, and most of the All A's and B's shouldn't have gotten a prize. Excellence should be recognized and rewarded, not mediocrity. This is recognizing authentic achievement and noting that it is special. The achievers are recognized and the other kids are given encouragement to do better. Also, kids aren't made to feel left out because only a few were recognized and rewarded.

Eventually this practice fell out of use, but it does pop up from time to time in various schools across the nation thanks to another phenomenon that occurs in all educational circles, group think. Watch out for that. It has the potential to ruin all kinds of things in life. The human need of achievement is definitely one of them.

Chapter 5 Self Actualization

Personal Growth

Growth of the soul - this is something we all want, but what exactly is it? I just put it in semi-religious terms, but that's just how I roll. Maslow was simply talking about being the best you can be. When all the other needs are met, one can look outside of himself. If you're going to be in the world, may as well make the best of it. Maybe you can even leave it a little better than the way you found it day by day. A wise person realizes that this doesn't happen by telling others what they're doing wrong. All this does is make your problems everybody else's problems too, which builds resentment and general unhappiness. Instead, you work on yourself and make yourself a good citizen. Fortunately, good citizenship can be, and often is, fostered in schools.

If self actualization is to be fostered in schools, it must first be valued. Many teachers do intuitively. This why they always tell students to do their best work. But they also foster good citizenship too. They praise good manners and thank kids for doing good things that they didn't have to do. Kids are appreciated for doing necessary chores or other good character actions without being asked. They recognize kids' natural talents and encourage their students to continue developing them.

Okay, here's a pet peeve of mine that I see other teachers doing all the time. It's not a big deal, but I don't understand why they do it. Sometimes kids finish their work early. Maybe they're working on a test in which all the papers are taken up at the same time. Some kids like to draw. There are a lot of teachers who reprimand their students for doing this. They tell them that they don't want to see their drawings on the papers. WHY ON EARTH WOULD YOU CARE? Let them doodle. Sure, they don't need to be rummaging around in their desks looking for other paper or art materials while the other students are testing. Granted, they don't need to draw on their test answers. I totally get that. But if there's empty space on the back or down at the bottom of the paper, and there almost always is, let them draw. Again, just a pet peeve of mine, but I sure wouldn't want to be the teacher that stopped the next Renoir from developing his skills (just kidding, sort of).

Administrators can foster a school environment that promotes and encourages self actualization at all levels.

Again, it's not about telling others what they're doing wrong. That's called being a jerk. It is about recognizing others' efforts authentically. That's called good leadership. The one piece of advice I can give to administrators is to, once again, be as genuine as possible. For example, over the past several years many of the higher ups in my school system have been sure to thank us for all that we do. It's nice of them. But sometimes, especially after a faculty meeting, I want to ask, "What did I do?" Of course I don't say that, because I would be totally out of line and my principal is just doing his/her job. There is an upshot to this stream of thought, though. Administrators, take notice of the good your faculty and staff are doing. You will in all likelihood discover that those good things will magically multiply.

One caveat to this citizenship idea. It is not political in nature. Nor should it be politicized. You don't become a better person by being an activist, especially if you're a kid. Right now, celebrities and pop culture would lead kids to believe that they have to have a pet political cause. The dirty little secret is that you can be a perfectly good person without trying to change society at large. All these pop stars peddling their political ideas are probably just trying to do something to feel better about themselves. There's nothing wrong with caring about issues. Likewise, there's nothing wrong with speaking your mind. I'm just saying that I'd much rather be around the kid (or adult for that matter) that picks up trash on the playground than the one that berates others for littering. That's self actualization in a nutshell. If you lead by example and give kids the opportunity to be better people, they almost always will.

Chapter 6 Why I Wrote This Book

A few years ago, I was listening to a podcast called Personality Hacker. I'm a big fan of the personality typing system called MBTI. The couple on this podcast use personality typing and other psychological models as maps and guides for self growth. I certainly don't agree with all that they have to say, but they really know their stuff. On one of these podcast episodes, they were talking about Disney World. They tried an interesting anecdotal experiment. In a parking lot outside the amusement park, they smiled and waved at some fellow tourists. Their reaction? They promptly ignored them and gave the impression that they thought they were crazy. Once inside the park, they waved at some other families, who immediately smiled and waved back. This was a stark difference. People's behaviors had turned around one hundred eighty degrees. The only difference was distance, less than half a mile. The podcasters attributed this phenomenon to Maslow's Hierarchy of Needs. They discussed how people were happier and so much more opened to others around them when all their needs were securely met. This, of course, is one of Disney's specialties. It got me to thinking.

A few years before, I had moved schools. The morale in that school had dropped dramatically. There is no need to discuss why or to lay blame on any one person. These things happen. But my daughters went to another school in which the environment was completely different. It was noticeable too. People were happier, just like in the Disney experiment. Sure, it was probably because of good leadership. But what was the nature of that leadership? What made it so much better? Being ever observant, I took note of different school settings. I was in a pretty good one, and thankfully I still am. But there were differences in morale between the schools. My teaching position is unique in that I get to see the whole school in multiple grade levels on a daily basis. I also get to talk to colleagues who travel between schools. Some schools, even in a well run system, are better than others. I began noticing the patterns. The schools with the lowest morale were having trouble meeting certain needs is Maslow's famous hierarchy.

Fast forward a few years later, and I had some time on my hands due to the COVID19 pandemic. Stuck at home, my kids kept me pretty busy and I was doing some "teleteaching," but I could always steal some time to write. Teachers think about their jobs a lot. This one decided to jot a few of those thoughts down.

Usually I prefer writing fiction. Writing nonfiction like this feels clunky and uneasy to me. In short, it's hard work. It doesn't flow like fictional stories. But I decided this was important. If there's an administrator out there who's wondering why he/she's having a hard time leading the school, this book may have some of those answers and provide some guidance. If there's a teacher out there who's about to give up on reaching his/her students. I think this short book can help. In other words, I wrote this book because I was following Abraham Maslow's advice. I'm meeting my own need of self actualization and trying to be a good citizen.

Finally, it must be said that any of the horror stories I wrote about in these pages were mostly one time occurrences, or at least short lived trends. It is easier to illustrate the importance of the needs on the hierarchy by showing what it looks like when they are not met. Most of the time in my school system, they are. I work in a great school that's in a great school system. People make mistakes. Some of the missteps I mentioned earlier were done by people that I have come to respect and even admire. And to be fair, I didn't mention any of my biggest blunders. Believe me, there are plenty.

Chapter 7   So?

Okay, your school has some problems. What do you do about it? I'm not even going to pretend I have all the answers. But the hierarchy can be useful. Begin the school year with a print out of it on your desk to use as a guide. This goes for administrators and teachers alike. If everyone has it handy, it will be in the forefront where it belongs. It can be accessed easily through that magical inter webs contraption. Heck, kick it up a notch and laminate it!

If you're an administrator that has to execute some new school policy, hold it up to the hierarchy. Ask yourself if any need in the hierarchy is being unmet or violated. If so, do something about that. Make it your personal educational constitution. You still have to meet the requirements of the higher ups in the district or state, but you can insure that the school's needs are met too. That's a win win. You have the power. You should imagine that last sentence in a Darth Vader voice.

Teachers, by no means should you use this when writing lesson plans. If your administrators think so, they have totally missed the boat. Believe me, this happens a lot.

Just look how Bloom's Taxonomy has been abused over the years. It is advisable, however, that you reflect on the hierarchy daily. Ask yourself if one of your rituals or routines are violating any of the needs. If so, adjust accordingly. Make your classroom a place where your students needs are met every day. Both you and your kids will be happier for it.

Grade level and faculty meetings are great places to use the hierarchy. After going through the usual process with your captive audience, administrators and team leaders should be open to any input from the faculty specifically concerning the needs. It's a lot better than the old, "Are there any questions?" question. The answer to that is a resounding (though eerily silent in nature) NO for everyone who wants to go home except that one person (you know who you are).

Small changes build up and mushroom over time. They reach a critical mass. This can be catastrophic, like with a nuclear explosion. But it can also be a wonderful thing too. Changes will come. Why not strive to make them as positive as possible? It's a way of shaping your school's destiny. And by default, it will change the lives of untold numbers of kids.

This brief work isn't meant to revolutionize education. If it were, someone else would have written it and it would have been much longer. It is simply meant to be a useful tool to help make things better in your school. Use it that way, and I truly believe things will change for the better over time. If every school in the nation does this, fantastic! If only one school does this or something like it, fantastic! The point is that the opportunity is there for the taking.

Printed in Great Britain
by Amazon